OMINOUS CRACKS

"Well —as far as I can make out what you lose upon the roundabouts you lose upon the swings." 30.iii.77

OMINOUS CRACKS

*

New Pocket Cartoons

by

OSBERT LANCASTER

JOHN MURRAY

1979

Osbert Lancaster's Other Works

PROGRESS AT PELVIS BAY
PILLAR TO POST
HOMES SWEET HOMES
A CARTOON HISTORY OF ARCHITECTURE
ALL DONE FROM MEMORY (Autobiography)
WITH AN EYE TO THE FUTURE (Autobiography)
SAILING TO BYZANTIUM
THE SARACEN'S HEAD
DRAYNEFLETE REVEALED
CLASSICAL LANDSCAPE WITH FIGURES
THE LITTLEHAMPTON BEQUEST
THE PLEASURE GARDEN (with Anne Scott-James)
SCENE CHANGES

Pocket Cartoons

SIGNS OF THE TIMES 1939–1961
MEANINGFUL CONFRONTATIONS
PRIVATE VIEWS
THEATRE IN THE FLAT
LIQUID ASSETS
THE SOCIAL CONTACT

Grateful acknowledgement is made to the Editor for kind permission to reprint the drawings which have appeared in the *Daily Express*.

Printed in Great Britain for John Murray, Albemarle Street, London, at The Pitman Press, Bath
0 7195 3683 9

"Some of you may have thought that the study of history serves no practical purpose." 14.iv.77

FOREWORD

In the sure conviction that no one ever reads a word of these forewords the temptation to indulge in wild libel or scabrous indecency, or both, is hard to resist. But as this opinion is not shared by my publisher—an optimistic, but apprehensive, type—I shall, as always, confine myself to a few quiet generalisations, banal but not actionable.

At the moment of writing we are all—or nearly all—caught up, or at least tactfully making a show of being so, in pre-election fever, but however eagerly the contestants and their loyal supporters may look forward to the contest, no one in their senses but must tremble at the thought of the stream of unconvincing, and frequently ungrammatical, rhetoric which is about to overwhelm us in the Press and on all channels, so it were better to confine oneself to the backward glance.

The end of the decade was marked by an outburst of sexual activity unparalleled, if one is to believe the newspapers, since the Cities of the Plain; octogenarian rapists vied with teenage Messalinas for a place in the headlines; transvestites and nymphomaniacs flourished in the most unlikely places, such as boardrooms, vestries and infant schools—or so we were assured. Krafft-Ebing, one felt, had died too soon.

Whether or not all this surprising outburst was due to increased leisure, or an improved diet, remains a matter for speculation, but certainly more people had more time on their hands than ever before. Many, even including a number of trendy clergymen, greeted this phenomenon as a perhaps in some ways regrettable, but nonetheless encouraging, sign of the abandonment of old and outworn prejudices and as a new freedom of the flesh reflecting a new liberation of the spirit. Others, more old-fashioned, felt that Satan had, as usual, found work for idle hands, if I may be allowed the euphemism, to do.

Meanwhile, everywhere the urban skyline was continuously enriched by soaring tower blocks, a large proportion of which remained conspicuously empty. The great festivals of the church, Christmas, Easter, Whitsun, as for that matter most secular holidays, were regularly marked by major breakdowns of public transport. Queues grew even longer until a point was reached when those at the tail had, by the time they gained the head, long since forgotten whether they were awaiting the take-off of Concorde, the 7.45 to Haywards Heath, or the last performance of *Swan Lake*. Some, but not all, derived comfort from the reflection that we were finally in Europe, even if the advantages of our inclusion were not perhaps immediately apparent. Throughout the period prosperity remained just around the corner, but unfortunately the corner itself continued to recede at an every increasing rate of knots.

April 1979 O. L.

"Could you, perhaps, let me have a solvent newspaper?"
27.iv.77

"My Dear, wonders never cease! Rees-Mogg has discovered sex at last, and doesn't like it!" 28.iv.77

"Don't tell me your mother sent you back without a slush fund!?" 24.v.77

"And what exactly is the trouble, Mrs Vickers?" 14.vi.77

"Excuse me –I'm on rather a sticky picket!" 22.vi.77

"Oh dear, what a terrible report! Three out of fifty for handicrafts and bottom in sex-play!" 29.vi.77

"Gay News." 5.vii.77

"Just what we don't want—what we need is a bomb that wrecks the architecture and spares the inhabitants!"
14.vii.77

"But why don't we hand Rhodesia over to Northern Ireland —or vice versa?" 26.vii.77

"No, no, no, Sir Charles! All I said was I was nervous lest we might be B-U-G-G-E-D!" 2.viii.77

"Do you remember, Uncle Longstop, telling us all about the sordid commercialism of professional football?"
5.viii.77

"Why can't the Government forget about outer space and pay a little more attention to S.W.1?" 15.ix.77

"Nil desperandum! We've already got the mini Concorde waiting on the drawing board!" 22.ix.77

"Are we quite, quite sure that we're not boosting inflation?" 23.ix.77

"In view of the grievous disappointment that your enforced absence would cause all opera lovers, I am prepared to bind you over for the duration of the *Ring*."
27.ix.77

"By the way, Fontwater, the Bishop wants to know how you would feel about a female curate?" 19.x.77

"Have you, by any chance, a short history of the Liberal Party?" 20.x.77

"Wake up, Filebrace! Don't you realise we're on strike!?" 9.xi.77

"Here we are again! Nappies, nappies, nappies!" 16.xi.77

"Please may I leave the room—I think I've been over tranquillised." 1.xii.77

"I think there must be some mistake—this one's been autographed by Edward Heath." 9.xii.77

"And how much is poison ivy?" 14.xii.77

"Strictly between ourselves, officer, I've a shrewd suspicion I've been brain-washed." 6.i.78

"Dear Mrs Rajagojollibarmi, if it weren't for the Race Relations Board I'd say you've revoked!" 10.i.78

"What I need is a couple of jokes that are fairly new, moderately clean, and quite untinged with racialism."
11.i.78

"How much will the Liberal Party pay me not to paint Jeremy Thorpe?" 13.i.78

"Please, sergeant, what do I do with an intoxicated diplomatic representative of a foreign power, smoking cannabis, indecently exposing himself, and parked on a double yellow line?" 18.i.78

"Of course, you can write to the European Court of Human Rights—but you realise, don't you, that you'll have to do it in French?" 20.i.78

"The Race Relations Board—quick!" 24.i.78

"Now, tell me frankly, bearing in mind the Nonconformist vote, how exactly would *you* levy a tax on sex?"
9.ii.78

"And where am I supposed to put this—and I don't want a funny answer!" 10.ii.78

"If Ted and Maggie don't make it up soon everyone will start saying there's more to this than meets the eye!"
15.ii.78

"Just a moment, dear! Do you want to be Daily Express nurse of the year or don't you?" 21.ii.78

"Now do us a Michelangelo." 22.ii.78

"There goes another of Mr Callaghan's silver linings."
1.iii.78

"You mark my words, any minute now they'll discover that nuclear radiation is terribly good for us, and up will go the rates!" 7.iii.78

"Do you *really* want to know Leyland's balance sheet for 1980?" 21.iii.78

"Don't tell me *they* came in on the quota." 22.iii.78

"How do you spell 'proletariat'?" 29.iii.78

"But I promise you, Auntie, that an Oscar has absolutely nothing to do with the late Mr Wilde." 6.iv.78

"Speaking as one whose family came over with the Conqueror, I feel that I'm not in a very strong position to talk about immigrants." 14.iv.78

"Now we don't want to be just a deceitful sex object when we grow up, do we?" 21.iv.78

"Customer wants to know where's the Neuters' bar?"
19.v.78

"My lords, speaking as an unsuccessful abortion . . ."
26.v.78

"Now tell me, which is the Soviet Embassy and which is the new town hall—or are you sharing?" 6.vi.78

"Darling, how wonderful! Do you know, something told me I should find you here!" 14.vi.78

"Can I help you?" 15.vi.78

"How do babies come? Quite honestly, darling, granny's no longer one hundred per-cent certain." 20.vii.78

"Don't say I said so, but I happen to know that their mother came out of a test tube!" 27.vii.78

"Now if you'll tell me who's going to be the next Pope I'll tell you *all* about Jeremy Thorpe!" 9.viii.78

"Well, one way or another, they've certainly got a lot to talk about!" 12.ix.78

"Let's look on the bright side, dear—it might have been Daimler's." 26.ix.78

"All things considered, Miss Tremolo, I think that just for tonight, we might perhaps be well advised to omit 'In a Persian Garden'." 7.xi.78

"Why do so many of our public figures feel the need, in moments of crisis, to express themselves in hopelessly out-dated slang?" 8.xi.78

"Hold it, darling, hold it!" 9.xi.78

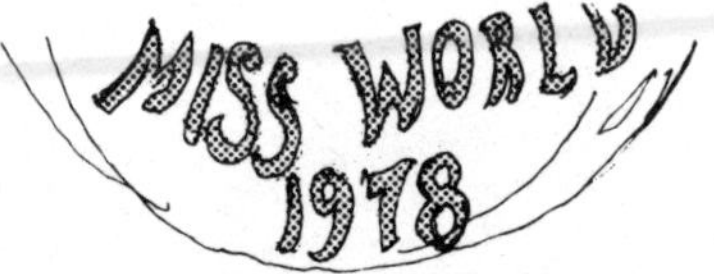

"The Misses Siam!" 17.xi.78

"Tell me Mrs Rajagojollibarmi, what are you sending Mrs Gandhi this Christmas?" 20.xii.78

"If you ask me, it's high time Women's Lib insisted on a Mother Christmas!" 22.xii.78

"Heavens above! Snow in JANUARY!" 3.i.79

"Why don't we just say 'Unidentified Flying Object' and leave it at that?" 4.i.79

"Would you like the news now or shall we save it to spoil our dinner?" 30.i.79

"You understand Sister? No more hernias while the crisis lasts!" 2.ii.79

"How many times has mother told you *not* to throw away your toffee papers in the street?!" 6.ii.79

"Come on, let's do something which would horrify Mrs Whitehouse—like having a bath!" 7.ii.79

"Mummy, darling, how come that you were never a Duchess of Westminster?" 20.ii.79